W.O.R.D.S.

Wisdom to Survival

ELIZABETH FABIEN

authorHOUSE®

AuthorHouse™
1663 Liberty Drive
Bloomington, IN 47403
www.authorhouse.com
Phone: 833-262-8899

Published by AuthorHouse 08/10/2022

ISBN: 978-1-6655-6729-9 (sc)
ISBN: 978-1-6655-6728-2 (e)

W.O.R.D.S.

Wisdom and Willingness
Objective and Obligation
Reason and React
Dream and Dare
Suffer and Survive

CONTENTS

Corner of Gratitude ix

W.O.R.D.S.: Corner of Self-realization, Positivity and Morality

Why? 1
The Alpha And Omega 3
It Was Meant To Be 4
The Two Extremes 5
The Two Extremes (Part II) 6
Lyfe Vs. A Circle 8
Dreams 10
Just A Thought 12
The Speech Of The Wise 13
State Of Mind 14
Success 16
Controversy 17
God And Religion 18
My Conversation With God 19
God Exists 20
Born Again 21

W.O.R.D.S.: Corner of Mystery

Joy, I Thought It Was Reality 25
The Vision 26
Mystery Of Life 27

W.O.R.D.S.: Corner of Love (Relationships)

Love 31
The Two Of Us 32
From Expectation To Resolution 33
The Two Love Birds 34
If Only Love Could Be 35
Love In The Dream 36

A Broken Heart.. 37

If I Take It Back... 38

Loving To Death.. 39

Once Upon A Time 40

Simple Request... 41

L'amour.. 42

You Were Not There.. 43

Love As A Flower 45

Is It Real? 46

I Miss You... 47

On That Day... 48

W.O.R.D.S.: Corner of Love (Humanity)

We Are One 51

Star 54

The Little Newborn Girl 55

My Mom.. 56

The Jungle Of Distress 57

W.O.R.D.S.: Corner of prophetic thoughts

The House...61

Slaves 62

Shift – Slaves Part II... 63

My First Sonnet 64

Freedom 65

The Spirit Of Our Ancestors 66

Inspired.. 67

We Will Get Back 69

So And So Is Poison 70

Stop Controlling Me… 73

God, You're Speaking...74

Parade Of Blessings With Only Eyes To See....................... 75

7/12 77

Final Thoughts.. 78

W.O.R.D.S. 81

CORNER OF GRATITUDE

I would like to thank the **Most High God** for being the leader of my life. All honor, praise and glory are to Him.

I would like to thank my Mom **Marie Claude** who has been playing a dual role in my life since the age of nine. She is the perfect meaning of true love and wisdom.

I would like to thank my family, especially my big brother **Jean Hebert Fabien**, aunts **Benita Fabien Bony** and **Ghyslaine Brillant**, uncles **Jimmy Bony** and **Thomas Michel Fabien,** cousins **Peggy Brillant** and **Catia Fabien** and her family and the rest of my relatives from Florida, New York, Massachusetts and Canada.

I would to thank my close friends from Bazz **Sophia Délone, Angella Germain, Monalissa Jean, Stephanie Germain, Vladimir Frederic** and **Tracy Bellevue.** My friends from Miami Dade College **Ann Jean Mary and family, Jokebed Dexiste, Lourna Demesie, Samantha Jeannot, Rhony Jean Simon, Harry Frezin, Amos Jean Glaude** and **Monyves Rousseau.**

I would like to thank my weekly support system **Joyce Onoré, Geraldine Lovince, Esthere Louis** and family, **Margaly Maxius Adam, Nikishia G. Pierre Tranquille, Jennifer Veillard Forest, Junon Fertil** and family, my mentors **Charlemont & Marlene Genestin, Teshler & Gierda Senat** and business partners and colleagues who all have supported me throughout the years.

Thank you to **Boukan** with Boukan Night, **Poetic Lakay**, and **Poetry & Talents** where friends like **Naomie Labaty, Angie Bell, Mecca Grimo Marcelin** and **Lesly Charles** have helped me expose my talents.

Special thanks to **Peterson Mead**, **Halfdan Osse** and **Ryshade Hyppolite** who have been avid supporters of my poetry throughout the years.

Thanks to **everyone** else near or far who made a difference in my life. You know who you are! This project would not be possible without you!

W.O.R.D.S

Corner of Self-realization, Positivity and Morality

In the short period of time that I have been on Earth, I have witnessed so many things. In the end, what I realize is that it all comes down to having a good relationship with God our creator, oneself and people. If we could all master these three simple words but yet complex concepts, the world would truly be a better place as often stated. This could lead to the birth of real change in our communities through willing leaders.

WHY?

Why can't **humans** be one in the name of the Lord?
Why, for defense, they always hold a sword?
Everyone's just hanging around
Why can't they live according to God's will?
As opposed to being assaulters ready to kill
God created us similar to HIM
In return, all we do is reject HIM

Why can't **we** accept others with their flaws?
Why aren't we in sync with our immutable laws?
Without working, we expect miracles
We're living a lifestyle worse than that of animals
Why is this way of being approved?
To the Almighty, it's an improper move
Between wrong and right, we should choose
A lot is at stake, we must play not to lose

Why do **you** think you know it all?
Before making your first step, you had to crawl
Why do you think you have it all under control?
God is your leading edge from body to soul
Many are the plans of men
God's plans prevail for on high He reigns

Why do **you** rush everything you do?
Just to show off
God only takes pleasure in the real you
A genuine heart with no filter, no bluff
Why do you compete with the wrong motive?
Or try hard to be a person of notice?
There's a season for everything
Give time for the champion in you to win

Why do people feel the need to follow a trend?
It comes and goes with a beginning and an end
It's your obligation to be your most authentic self
To live a life with a mind and pocket full of wealth

Why does he judge a book by its cover?
Without even reading a page or summary
Meanwhile, he's living his life undercover
With guilt and shame seeking to be free
So many questions needing an answer
And the world left to figure
Why?

HIGHLIGHT

Why can't **humans** be one in the name of the Lord?
Why, for defense, they always hold a sword?
Everyone's just hanging around
Why can't they live according to God's will?

03-05-05

THE ALPHA AND OMEGA

As the world turns, many people are starting to realize that there's really a MAN above; He is GOD, the Almighty

Life is given to us according to His grace, that's why he is the GIVER of LIFE

For all these blessings, he deserves all the praise and glory; we should worship him wholeheartedly

Amen, as we say every day is for acceptance and belief

Only He knows who and what we truly are, where we came from and why we are put in this world

Most of the things we're able to see, creatures like ourselves, animals are under his obedience

Even the invisible is under his control

God is great, he is the Alfa, the Omega, the beginning and the end

And we should follow his will until the end

08-01-05

IT WAS MEANT TO BE

Eras have passed by and earthlings are existent
And the kingdom above reigns over them
It oversees everybody's act
And provides a heavenly feedback
There the door opened up for an opportunity
No timing, no clear purpose, let idea fly
When the perfect time comes around
Bodies will come out the ground
And answer to the Most High
It was meant to be
Everything seen, done and said has a purpose
In the book of life of the kingdom above
No need to set the mind against this
It was all because of love

HIGHLIGHT

**"When the perfect time comes around
Bodies will come out the ground
And answer to the Most High
It was meant to be"**

7-16-12

THE TWO EXTREMES

If not the negative, the positive side
So hated by many people, why?
Come to the front line, or hide
Don't reject it unless you try
Spend your money the right way
Everything's vanity, things come and go
Don't wait for tomorrow, TODAY IS THE DAY
Count on a Yes and count on a No
Disappointment is a part of life
Satisfaction will come along
Food's ready, set of spoon, fork and knife
Mood swings from weak to strong
The garden's dry, rain shall come
To bless the land, the old Eden
Will get several, many or some
From beginning until end
The world is upside down
We need the right side up
We just go square or round
Without setting up
We have visions to change
But in turn we destroy
Too much sadness is strange
The world is left to enjoy...

HIGHLIGHT

"Don't wait for tomorrow, TODAY IS THE DAY"
03-29-09

THE TWO EXTREMES (PART II)

We have visions to change
But in turn we destroy
Too much sadness it's strange
The world's left to enjoy
Enjoyed by ignorant blinded people
People called names or maybe Taínos
Their eyes don't serve them to see
To see the whole raw reality
I don't need any imagery
Let the spirit in me guide me
The basket is filled with berries
Half is good, half is spoiled
Take the top, make them your goodies
Let the bottoms be boiled
Upset your stomach not
The sentence is too strong
For the well-arranged plot
Done by those is so wrong
You are so innocent
Know this, please notice this
You are so ignorant
Open your eyes please see this
This is not your home
It is too filthy, too dirty
Remember where you come from
On the inside, you're pretty
Don't let that beauty fade
If so, never to be found again
Let your mouth be a blade
Speak while you can
Let our anger be abstained
So we do not destroy
Let our vision help us change
The world for us to enjoy

HIGHLIGHT

"This is not your home
It is too filthy, too dirty
Remember where you come from
On the inside, you're pretty"

03-23-10

LYFE VS. A CIRCLE

Lyfe takes shape in a circle
That trains thee and makes thee act the same
You go to sleep, wake up, and follow the same goal
Lyfe surely has an aim
Lived in the past
Is oddly living in the present
Has no need to ask
And never seems to be absent
Who is Lyfe?
Lyfe is this largely giving person
Who gives without a reason…
Simply because giving is loving
And loving a reason to give
Everything that Lyfe does
Has done it sometime before
Everything that Lyfe gives
Wants to give more
Everything is happening inside the circle
A dot as starting point
The same dot as ending point
Lyfe walks on that path
For it is defined and written
Not three fourth nor half
But the whole ten
Lyfe can't tell you
Unless you want to find out
The unknown and so called truth
That you are all about
Lyfe gives you a sign as you take your guess
Be kind and do the rest

HIGHLIGHT

"Lyfe is this largely giving person
Who gives without a reason...
Simply because giving is loving
And loving a reason to give"

10-25-07

DREAMS

Dreams, dreams, dreams
I have so many
Hidden behind the door
Like the different teams
I'm trying to score
Points to win
The battle that life is
Before my own ceases
Almighty, step in

Dreams, dreams, dreams
I have so many
Hidden behind the door
Knocking constantly
Within myself there's a war
Two-sided with good and evil
Away from me, they are fading
At the deepest level
To the Almighty I'm praying

Dreams, dreams, dreams
I have so many
Hidden behind the door
I'm looking for my key
To step on the other side
Hands-on they shall be
Neither I nor they can hide
And the world shall see

HIGHLIGHT

"I'm trying to score
Points to win
the battle that life is
Before my own ceases
Almighty step in"

JUST A THOUGHT

It is good to want to follow one's footsteps for guidance and direction but what is not ok is to strive to be someone we are not. As a society, we are so conditioned to living the lives of others that we forget to live our own or so caught with copying other people's identity that we forget to carve our own. We get trapped by pleasing people and their selfish desires while we lose ourselves in the process. There is a limitless possibility for one to be the truest version of self without having to fit with others.

THE SPEECH OF THE WISE

As you wake up today
Get on your knees and pray
Thank God for this new day of birth
As unexpectedly, you see yourself on Earth
Be cautious on your way out
Don't forget the ones you care about
Use your past as a reference to change your present
See other's success as a movement
Live according to nature
NOW is the time to plan your future
Learn to lose before you can win
It's not a sin, but life's routine
Prove wrong only when you have the right answer
Everyone deserves a chance to get better
Love the ones who care about you
Do whatever you want to be done to you
Live each day like it's your last
Do not waste time for it runs fast
Make sure you look good within
Between you and Joe the line is thin
Do not judge a book by its cover
The shame will be your subject matter
Do everything life demands you to
In due time, your success will come through

HIGHLIGHT

**"Live each day like it's your last
Do not waste time for it runs fast"**

STATE OF MIND

Sun is down and it's up, breathing routine
Wipe face, sit down, think and think again
Fight of the human from deep within
It is so gone to the unknown place of sin
Nothing left to do, follow the daily path
That the Rabbi once did in so many days
Discourage not, full the opposite of half
Rewards to come in several ways
Act just in the eyes of the Holy One
For the feeding bread of daily breath
Wake up, talk, and walk, greet someone
Wrong or right shall cometh death
Sun is down and it's up, breathing routine
Fight of the human from deep within

HIGHLIGHT

"Sun is down and it's up, breathing routine
Fight of the human from deep within"

02-01-09

For some success is inevitable based on their background and heritage but for others it requires climbing harder steps in the ladder to reach the feat. Success becomes this foreign language one strives to speak. Here are some concepts and principles amassed throughout the years that have helped me understand and continue to learn this language.

"Believing in others is often easy; it's believing in yourself that's the real challenge" ~Elizabeth Fabien

"It's all about mastering people and you are one of them" ~Elizabeth Fabien

"As you're working towards being a better leader for others; you must focus on being a better leader for yourself" ~Elizabeth Fabien

"The prerequisite to helping others is helping you first" ~Elizabeth Fabien

"Be at peace with the fact that if it is to be it's up to you" ~Elizabeth Fabien

"Your success may be delayed but not denied. God is just preparing you for your moment; so embrace the learning curves" ~Elizabeth Fabien

"Don't focus on the glory, just build your story" ~Elizabeth Fabien

"It's not about the title but about the person you become in the process" ~Elizabeth Fabien

"Each achievement marks not a destination but a step in the journey" ~Elizabeth Fabien

"Keep up the grind, get better every day and success will be waiting for you" ~Elizabeth Fabien

Fabien Quotes

SUCCESS

Success leads an individual to stability
We usually want to live to see, to do and let it be.
In this world, all of us want to succeed
We want to be the ones in the lead
Success is about setting goals to make it in life
And knowing what to do to not just get by
Life is not simple; life is hard, but also beautiful
Take this opportunity in the truth to be fruitful
Success means wanting to go further, not giving up
All about going for the best; without a stop
If you put effort into your own goals
You'll realize that it's for a fighter like yourself
Without asking, let in two ways be your wealth
Success is all that you can dream for
It's all about wanting more and more
Against yourself, do not let it be a war
Just let it determine who you truly are

HIGHLIGHT

"Success means wanting to go further, not giving up
All about going for the best; without a stop"

CONTROVERSY

It is so difficult to understand the meaning of life
To also understand why we breathe, sneeze and sigh
The concepts of inferiority and superiority
The difference between wrong and right
The one between darkness and light

It is always said that feelings come from the heart
Experts suggest that everything is based on our thoughts
The fact of relying on old facts is set on our mind by default
This one which is like a computer performing the art

If we start seeing things in a different color
Such as expanding our mind to another level
We will realize that the world has so much to offer
We prefer to be late for the good and early for the bad
By the time we open our eyes, it is all over

Do you know that you actually have to be smart to play the dumb role?
Or to succeed in life, you need to focus on the main goal?
Or to gain something, you definitely have to lose?
And to not be disappointed, you just have to choose?

HIGHLIGHT

**"If we start seeing things in a different color
Such as expanding our mind to another level
We will realize that the world has so much to offer"
11-15-05**

GOD AND RELIGION

I have built the culture and trait that following a religion is not as important to me as having a relationship with God. Some are ritualistic while others just operate by the spirit. I have a non-denominational faith. I have had countless encounters with God where He has not only revealed himself to me but has also delivered me from the works of the enemy. He has brought healing to my body as well as my spirit. With this alone, I know that He does exist.

MY CONVERSATION WITH GOD

God, what should I do to be saved?
What should I do so that my way can be paved?
Well my dear! night and day you should pray
Follow my commands for I am the way
Have faith in me, for I am the key to salvation
Do not let your mediocrity pay for your action
Forgive and forgiveness shall be yours
Help your brother; it is for a good cause
Unseal your lips to propagate my word
To your environment and to this lost world
Be pure for you are my servant
Everything thrown will be caught if in my name it is sent
I will use you to heal your brother
Through your prayer, I will spread my power
You shall be CONFIDENT
Believe that the blessing will be given
Let my words become your food
Abstract yourself from being rude
Whatever you do, always think of me
If you apply all these rules, dear child, salvation shall be

HIGHLIGHT

"Have faith in me, for I am the key to salvation
Do not let your mediocrity pay for your action"

GOD EXISTS

He supervises the world day by day
He controls the many steps that we take
He does not judge us by our mistakes
But analyzes the words we say
He created us a land filled with products
So we can be fed everyday
All kinds of animals from birds to ducks
They're also fed the same way
Days like Monday through Sunday
Months of 30, 31 days like January and May
The sun rises and it sets
We have houses, cars and jets
Roads, mountains and hills
Water for many purposes
Oxygen to breathe
And finally the nature to live
What a great gift given to us!
Even more like his son Jesus
God truly exists; his love is unconditional
His love is indeed unconditional!

HIGHLIGHT

**"What a great gift given to us!
Even more like his son Jesus"**

07-03-05

BORN AGAIN

I am born again
After years of pain
Like a baby I'm out of the womb again
God has given me a second chance
To live the life I am starting to understand
I am born again
Today I am not the same
Because God is leading my lane
I am born again
I understand the Man of men
Who's guiding my current season…
Who's telling me I can
I am born again
I understand that I'm only human
That I should let some things happen
For inexplicable reasons
I am born again
I know the definition of I can
I know where I stand
I am born again
No more pain within

HIGHLIGHT

**"Today I am not the same
Because God is leading my lane"**

09-11-07

W.O.R.D.S

Corner of Mystery

JOY, I THOUGHT IT WAS REALITY

After closing my eyes and falling deeply asleep
I ventured myself into an extreme sleep
A puff of wind led me to this other world
Where there is no fear, beef nor quarrel

I was taken to a place called "source of joy"
Visualizing all the things I could enjoy
Didn't know where I was but wanted to stay
So amazed, like a mute, nothing could I say

To describe someone's mood sad was no longer used
People were taught to compassionate not to accuse
Even, it was on each side, no more win or lose
Plenty were the opportunities for one to choose

The statement "do or die" wasn't used anymore
Caring, loving, embracing and so much more
People were not allowed to get mad
The good was there to outweigh the bad

Opening eyes from an out of nowhere noise
Wake up! Wake up! An unknown person's voice
It was a dream, it is all over
I guess good things don't last forever
Where am I? Back to misery
Joy, I thought it was reality!

HIGHLIGHT

The statement "do or die" wasn't used anymore
Caring, loving, embracing and so much more
People were not allowed to get mad
The good was there to outweigh the bad"

THE VISION

Resuming a few seconds of sleep
With the mean of that side
And some brown old sheet
In my comfortable ride
Here is what I see
A double-sided colored sky
Made of darkness and light
A mountain raised up high
And a man sitting alone in the night
Sobbing head facing down
It was the ultimate of many rounds
I saw a black crown
A complete silence, no sounds
A womanish hair
A face of despair
And I woke up….

02-23-10

MYSTERY OF LIFE

Something as unexplainable
As the pieces behind a riddle
The confusion, the fear within you
The discoveries of the new
Coded matters make life a mystery
Its contents, its concepts
The issues we happen to neglect
Our ups and downs
Laugh and cries
Truth and lies
Problems and difficulties
Tasks and duties
Our diverse responsibilities
The different boundaries

Leave it all up to God
It is not what you can do
But what God can do for you
Through the power of prayer
Through knowing him as your savior
The power of the air is the devil
Bring your faith to another level
Pray with confidence
To experience God's presence
And minimize strife
In this mystery of life

HIGHLIGHT

**"It is not what you can do
But what God can do for you"**

10-26-05

W.O.R.D.S

Corner of Love

(Relationships)

I have a love and hate relationship with the subject of love. Nevertheless, it is so good to love no matter the amount of deceptions and heartbreaks you may go through along your walk in life. Your parents, your peers, that someone and people from your entourage are made to be loved and appreciated. As a human being, I have come to realize that we tend to extend our love to those we feel are deserving of it; but God, in his mercy, demonstrated the greatest act of love in Jesus as a sacrificial lamb for the sins of mankind.

LOVE

(The basis of everything on earth)

Love was there before our existence
It is the reason why we're living
God simply formed a sentence
Here we are together breathing
Love can be sometimes incredible
In a way timing and predictable
Love was said to be blind
It is truly a feeling of one kind
Everyone perceives love their own way
It's just an emotion that can't be taken away

HIGHLIGHT

**"Love was there before our existence
It is the reason why we're living"**

THE TWO OF US

Just the two of us in a relationship
A step one level above friendship
Only God knows the future of our togetherness
Our goal should have us bringing the other happiness
Not letting anyone interfere between us
Loving each other at no cost
Being as truthful as we can be
Purposefully improving our personality
Devotion should be a part of what we share
That will make our problems easier to bear
We have God, the Holy Spirit, and Jesus
Bust as a couple, it will always be the two of us

11-02-05

FROM EXPECTATION
TO RESOLUTION

From a wish of mine
An expectation seeming to last a lifetime
Came to resolution
Under such a tension
An outing to the movies was the idea
To the famous mall of Aventura
Finally, there we were alone
Making love the theme of our song
On a Saturday night, unlike the others
Looking for what might reunite two old lovers
Nice words into my ears
Those I haven't heard in years
So moving they brought tears
While releasing all my fears
A wet kiss after a please
Lighted our hearts
Mouth to mouth, no release
Knowing so well our parts
In your arms, I wanted to stay
With you, was hoping to fly away
That's when I realized that I love you
Day by day, I'm getting closer to you
With God, our sole leader
I know our love will grow stronger

HIGHLIGHT

"Nice words into my ears
Those I haven't heard in years
So moving they brought tears
While releasing all my fears"

THE TWO LOVE BIRDS

I am so proud of them
It's been a while since they've been flying
They started their journey in a city in the south
Their destination is unknown
But their flight is still on the roll
The two love birds
I am so proud of them
For the friendship between them
Though they have lost wings while flying
They've still managed to heal come Spring season
Man! I enjoy watching these birds fly
Sometimes they make me wanna cry
Just to see the chemistry
Puts me close to reality
I am so proud of these love birds
I'm happy that their whistles can still be heard
I'm hoping that my bird could fly with me as well

Bird: referred to as friend
10-14-06
Dedicated to Ann & Hensley Moïse. They have been together for 17 years, married with 2 children.

IF ONLY LOVE COULD BE

I wish that love was sometimes optional
That one could just decide to love
But the supreme being from above
Made it somehow natural
The path that makes one an individual
Is so hard it can lead to suicide
But if love in its power is a guide
Then let suicide not be a goal
Love itself gives beauty to our existence
That same love can destroy our confidence
From what I've heard and what I've seen
From what was said and where I've been
Love is love but sometimes isn't love
So immense, it becomes uncontainable
But the supreme being from above
Made it somehow acceptable
Let my wish for love not be what I want it to be
For love is a natural feeling
Let love be what it is destined to be

HIGHLIGHT

"The path that makes one an individual
Is so hard it can lead to suicide
But if love in its power is a guide
Then let suicide not be a goal"

11-10-06

LOVE IN THE DREAM

If loving is wrong, what could possibly be right?
Is it caring and understanding? Please tell me
Is there a purpose for living the darkest life?
In ample hope of seeing the light?
Suffering at its deepest when the sun's up
Its lowest when it's down
It sends its rays, then sleeps at night
I dream of flame of fire burning my heart
I see ashes and a weak soul longing
For love; the plea of a torn apart
The dream is not over…
If only I could see what I want to see
Caring and understanding are what's left to offer
They both define what love means to me

HIGHLIGHT

**"Is there a purpose for living the darkest life?
…In ample hope of seeing the light?"**

06-13-11

A BROKEN HEART

In the dream was a broken heart
On the floor the remaining pieces
Life is full of surprises
As today she was torn apart

Desperate was the look on her face
And the unusual mood of the day
In her thoughts she went far away
Intentionally asking God for grace

In her mind were many secrets
That had her bothered and sad
Inside of her were laying regrets
That some may have never had

In the dream was a broken heart
On the floor the remaining pieces
Life is full of surprises
As today she was torn apart

IF I TAKE IT BACK

If I take it back to that month of the year
I'll have a chance to end up with a tear
But I'll try hard not to
Because it's already not worth it to be with you
A warm presence filled my life with joy
Just like a child receiving a toy
It was all I could ever dream for
Without knowing that there could be more
My life at this point was fulfilled
I was the lucky one in the lead
The dominant player on the field
If I can remember
It would be your touch, your eyes
The way you talk, your funny demeanor
I loved all of that
I can't lie about it
But now I'm in the present
All I can think about is a new scent
To put me on the right track
So I don't ever have to take it back

HIGHLIGHT

**"A warm presence filled my life with joy
Just like a child receiving a toy
It was all I could ever dream for
Without knowing that there could be more"**

12-17-06

LOVING TO DEATH

You never realize how deep you love someone
Until it's time to forgive and move on
You ask yourself; was I right or wrong?
Did he want to be with me for that long?
Is my heart guiding me or my instinct?
Will my boat come out of the sea or just sink?
These concerns best describe "loving to death"
Also the greatest feeling on our dear Earth
A connection made by God between two hearts
Sharing a special bond that no one can thwart
The simplicity of love starts with a friendship
The deeper you love leads to a relationship
It makes you want to wake up and live
Though you may not have much to give

HIGHLIGHT

"The simplicity of love starts with a friendship
The deeper you love leads to a relationship"

ONCE UPON A TIME

Eyes still open; dark in the morning
Insomnia from a sweet talk session
Fingers out, letters in, words shall sing
The verses of the song of emotion
22 days after New Year, number then my age
Everlasting prayer, inconsistent dream
Decisive feedback from divine cage
The muscle beating, sounds like art
Remark the feeling, not just a habit
It is the real fruit of forgiveness
Sincerity and patience define it
Smooth and effortless process
The eye, the heart, the target, and yes I do
Is my new way of saying I love you

HIGHLIGHT

"Fingers out, letters in, words shall sing
The verses of the song of emotion"

Written in 2008

SIMPLE REQUEST

The flood came once, twice ravaged my heart
Now I'm standing in the Dark
You're up North, I'm down South; we're apart
We're the last on Earth like Noah, I will build my arc
To your side of the world, I will arrive
Where the Lord saved a spot for you and I
No mornings yet but soon the sun will rise
For the book written for our lives does not lie
Like the waves of the sea led by the good spirit
Let our source of intention be a reason to live
No swearing, symbolizing, let us be legit
Let the flood cease and vice versa our love to give
There I will be standing in the Light
And the tunnel will shine in the middle of the night

HIGHLIGHT

"No swearing, symbolizing, let us be legit
Let the flood cease and vice versa our love to give"

01-29-10

L'AMOUR

Puis-je dire aujourd'hui
Que l'amour est plus fort que la mort
Demain pourtant tu m'en feras tort
L'amour n'a pas de prix
C'est quelque chose de gratuit
Il se laisse prendre par qui il veut
Surtout par celui ou celle qui le mérite
Il marche sur un lent rythme
Comparable à celui d'une tortue
Il est patient et quelquefois tue
Dépendamment du temps mis
Il se soumet et est soumis
Puisque son seul bien est par ici
Il se demande que faire pour enfin être fier
Il se fait du souci
Même qu'il soit gratuit
Il se montre conservatif
Pourtant est de nature expressif
Que faire de l'amour?
Lui donner son dernier tour
Est-ce que l'amour est sincère
Est-ce que "l'amour" veut vraiment faire
Je me demande mais je n'en sais rien

HIGHLIGHT

**"L'amour n'a pas de prix
C'est quelque chose de gratuit"**

01-24-07

YOU WERE NOT THERE

I recalled once at home
I was feeling alone
On a lazy day
So I found a way
To stay alive
By watching a show live
All that, was the subject of me expecting you
An evening I wanted to spend with you
I have searched every corner, everywhere
Consequently you were not there
A part of me was in sorrow
It was hidden in my face
I couldn't wait for tomorrow
To handle this case
You were not there
I was lost, so lost
The pain was within me
I didn't know what it would have cost
To have you beside me
I didn't know what to do
Than only ask for you
Unfortunately, you were not there
When I needed you the most
Dreaming of the day you would make a toast
And make us an official pair
Of your throne make me an heir
But you were not there

HIGHLIGHT

"I was lost, so lost
The pain was within me
I didn't know what it would have cost
To have you beside me"

04-01-05

LOVE AS A FLOWER

My love spreads like a flower grows in a garden
It needs liters of water to blossom
Once summer's here, dies now and then
Hot season's gone for others to come
Feelings becomes as cold as ice in winter
Neither sun nor water to flourish the heart
Nature in question facing dead flower
Like the NASA, response is about to depart
To fall in the sweet arms of who knows
At a destination predicted so unknown
The spirit of it comes, sees, and then goes
Until nature in question try to succumb
Nevertheless, flower still spreads abundantly
As long as natural rain falls daily

IS IT REAL?

From the first time you looked at me
To the time you held my hands
Till the time you last spoke to me
You left me mesmerized
I am craving one more gaze from your eyes
A sweet hug of hypnotize
Another sound to set my body on the rise
You inspire me to let go once more
And my muse has regained its core
The Man above
Refilled the fountain of love
Made it so pure, so real
Ready to accept and heal
Is it real?

02-22-17

I MISS YOU

If the sky seems to be distant to the sea
It shouldn't be the same between you and me
Your absence has me bathing in misery
Day after day, broader is the pain within me

My soul is claiming your presence
And my heart suffers during your absence
Here I am cultivating this anxiety
Without knowing what's happening to me

My desire is to love you more
In a way it has never been before
I feel guilty and do not know why
In a cocoon, all I can do is cry

Every moment with you is cherished
For your energy is sincere and pure
Every kiss given to you is treasured
For my heart smiles to you as it pours

HIGHLIGHT

**"My desire is to love you more
In a way it has never been before"**

01-01-05

ON THAT DAY

It doesn't take much to love or open up to the unlimited possibility of connecting to our source of energy.

As the universe reveals itself more and more humans become immune to its resources as a core.

For years, we have been accustomed to living by default ignorant to this existing reality being lived in this vault.

But in this day and age inquiring minds are wandering if reality isn't still left for discovery.

With that said, I've never been so emotionally ready to exercise the greatest feeling from the Man above in the form of love.

I want to love faithfully and vulnerably of a love that knows no boundaries

They say that experience is life's best teacher of lessons needed to get better

I will focus on that little voice while triaging for the right choice

Loving someone is as wonderful as an act and as powerful as a social impact

I pray that my journey brings exciting adventures and a better outcome for me.

01-15-2021

W.O.R.D.S

Corner of Love

(Humanity)

WE ARE ONE

Whatever race, ethnicity or background
From the poorest to the richest town
Black, White, Latino, same mitochondrial DNA
We were all conceived the same way
We are all from one mother
Call him brother; call me sister, we'll answer
We all have five fingers in our hands
We come from the original sand
The same blood runs through our veins
Cut me, cut her, we feel the same pain
We were put on Earth generation after generation
We're all here for a mission
We have three original ideas
We tend to have the same schemas
We have qualities and flaws
We are led by commands, rules and laws
We may not be royalties or comic actors
But we acquire our titles through our majors
No matter the religion, One God we serve
For what we do determines what we deserve
We have gifts acquired from the Great
We shall all walk through one Gate
We procreate and create our own
With our offspring, we have a bond
We were, are and will still be one
Our sins were washed away through the son
So we are One!
Inspired by my brother Jean Hebert Fabien

HIGHLIGHT

"We were sent down on Earth by the GREAT
When the TIME comes, we shall walk through one gate"

03-22-09

Sexual abuse is a taboo subject in our society. The unfortunate individuals who have brutally suffered from the aforementioned often lack the courage to come forward not only for help but also for healing. I had the privilege of working on several projects with a nonprofit organization dealing with cases of sexually assaulted victims. It was an amazing and instructive experience that led to the inspiration of this piece.

STAR

A star, you are a star
Lighted in the furthest side of the universe
Connected so far
To a land of so much more

A star, you are a star
A good spirit went wrong
Somewhere within a war
Lift your head up as you hear this song

A star, you are a star
A brand new one born today
No matter what they say
You're beautiful as you are

A star, you are a star
Way up there with a destiny
Peace settled with war
Go shine your light brightly

HIGHLIGHT

**"Peace settled with war
Go shine your light brightly"**

Written in 2013

THE LITTLE NEWBORN GIRL

She opens her eyes and greets the world
Asks for understanding with her fist in the air
I think she's probably in a dream

The room just met a little girl
The visitors came, each got a chair
I think they are part of the team

Plenty of tears, joy for the pearl
Filled with emotions a mother can't bear
I think she's probably in the dream

News spread like tattletale
Visitors, doctors, pictures everywhere
I think they are part of the team

Pretty facial features for a beautiful pearl
Looking up and down to what's out there
I think she is still in a dream

Time has come to rest little newborn girl
Visitors can now return their chair
I think that they are part of the team
That made up her dream

05-20-08

MY MOM

She is the most important treasure of my life
In the movie, she plays the role of great wife
She has seen me come out of the womb
At hospital *"Asile Français"* in that room
She fed me as a new newborn baby
Took care of me with safety
She loves me more than anything in this world
Was happy when I came out a girl
She is my mom, my heart, I adore her
And I am proud to call her mother
She's the one who never betrays me and never will
The one who loves me still
She gives me advice whenever I need some
She knows the pain when I feel one
I don't know what I could give inside
To always have her by my side
She is the best person I've ever known
My comfort when I am alone
For she knows me like the Father knows us
After God, the person in whom I put my trust
I, too, love her more than anything
And loving her is the best of all feelings

HIGHLIGHT

**"She gives me advice whenever I need some
She knows the pain when I feel one
I don't know what I could give inside
To always have her by my side"**

THE JUNGLE OF DISTRESS

Hunter for more, author for less
Heart beating hour after hour
Provoking a continuous stress
Teary eyes, shadow to cover
The dog kicked the bucket
He, who loved my bones,
Barking, waiting, mouth wet
Those days are so gone
Left behind memory trace
Hidden by snow and all
He sought the ideal place
Eyes can only visit the wall
Black mourning style left a heart
Go on my dog, make the Chart

01-20-09
Dedicated to my Stepfather who died on 12-17-08
Rest in peace Papy Joe

W.O.R.D.S

Corner of prophetic thoughts

I do not pretend to be a prophet but I do believe that I have a prophetic gift. It took the focus on writing in diverse styles, for various reasons in different seasons to realize that perhaps God wants to use my hands to share some enlightening messages to the world. This segment is made of revelations and inspired pieces that have been reluctant to share for years. As you read the latter, understand that these points of views are not reflecting a particular person or system but rather societal traits that have surged based on a lack of self-awareness or self-worth on the part of the oppressed or the mentally enchained.

THE HOUSE

On earth the reigning kingdom of lie
The avid object is watching so avidly
The house is made of tiles and an eye
Where so many eyes are so blurry
The house is for everyone
A spare for compensation
Based on the doctrine of one
Under a plain operation
One day the house shall fall
The eye shut
Facing the tangible result
Of the truth on the wall

HIGHLIGHT

"The house is for everyone
A spare for compensation"

08-08-2009

SLAVES

I am not a preacher
I am just the mouth
Delivering the message
We are slaves
Descendant of slaves
From the ancient time
Born in the system
Living in the system
Possibly dying in the system
This type of war and
"That" that is washed
Is shutting the light in our eyes
Closing and opening, same effect
Open your eyes and allow them to see
The lies before us
We are living in modern slavery
The indispensable tools have replaced
The ropes and physical tortures
Open our eyes
Modern slavery
Why are we requesting it?
The best people are being deceived
What for?
Help me answer

HIGHLIGHT

**"We are slaves
Descendant of slaves
From the ancient time
Born in the system
Living in the system
Possibly dying in the system"**

**10-27-09
To be continued...**

SHIFT – SLAVES PART II

It's there we don't see it
By the time we realize
It will be too late
Let ourselves be controlled
Demand for the things
Be part of the whole
Great deals are being made
Nobody cares, now and then a trade
Invasion in play for us
Our space, identity
We are worth just the dust
Open our eyes folks
TIME IS NOW
Plant seeds, let them grow
Teach kids, our own
What is there to know?
My heart is saddened
Because of what I see
But strengthened
In what is fed to me

HIGHLIGHT

**"TIME IS NOW
Plant seeds, let them grow"**

10-07-09

MY FIRST SONNET

From the desert to the side of the sea
The path of Negro man was so long
Like the multitude of slaves seeking liberty
The good sense and courage came along
Water, water, water, trace of miracle
Savior for the predator of freedom
Push away that brutal obstacle
And lead Negro man home
Rough, rough and tough road
Filled with spines, rocks and animals
Ice, Ice, ice it's so cold
Negro man needs to reach his goal
Pity for Negro man the seeker
Who never ever says never

05-09-08

FREEDOM

The body's here, the spirit gone
In the land of malicious deeds
No sword to fight let war come
Fulfill request of devil's needs
Concentrated tears, anticipation near
Long wanted freedom, slave to king
Thy shalt cometh, the ultimate year
Joy to the heart, slave will sing
Push away thy temptation, strength be here
Spirit new, free, free from devil
No more worries, not one tear
Option of thousand, chose to rebel
Long wanted freedom, slave to king
Joy to the heart, slave will sing

02-02-09

THE SPIRIT OF OUR ANCESTORS

We are living in the spirit of our ancestors
Being nice and rude existed before
Go on pursue these preexisting endeavors
The spirit of life wants you so much more

We are living in the spirit of our ancestors
Our bodies help the mechanical process
Out of nowhere, she's writing these scriptures
Perfect fit, perfect picture for spirits to address

We are living in the spirit of our ancestors
Past from terrestrial, sea creatures, and then people
We think, think and think again, we're thinkers
One Spirit for the first last and the middle

We are living in the spirit of our ancestors
Nothing is new; the world goes round and round
We dream of them in the world of protectors
The spirits are living; the sand is on the ground

04-08-09

INSPIRED

Slavery is the seed of all failure
Why do we suffer?
Is it a given right?
Or just a passage from darkness to light
The bulk of humanity has not yet realized
This complex puzzle called life
We go through generations
And we never master
The real concepts of daily living
We are given a pool of abundance
Which we reject with excuses
Because Mr. Ignorance is prevailing
Hmm.....Mr. Ignorance
Our brain is filled with bruises
Many injuries from battling
With forces of evil
Who's going to cry it out?
Who's going to go about
Getting us out of the hole?
Time to materialize the goal
Who's going to do us the many favors?
So needed to live in this world
Where are you (rare pearl)?
Pearl of freedom
Are you expensive? This we know
But with our sweat, you've been paid for
Mister Ignorance just can't leave
Because it's trapped in our sleeve
Who's going to change us except for us?
Let's wake up from that sleep
That the enemy has silently put us to
The others, the world and you too

Let's get to the hundred percentage
Free ourselves from lingering bondage
So we can see the face of the holy
Speak our prayers in clarity
Let us redefine our intention
Behind our words, put actions
So we can empower
The movement we are in
Let battle begin

HIGHLIGHT

**"Mister Ignorance just can't leave
Because it's trapped in our sleeve"**

09-16-13

WE WILL GET BACK

Oh yes we will!
To the original place
Where it all began
Where the "plus side only" prevails
It is all in the Earth what one needs
To unveil the mask of impossibility
Little by little, earthlings will climb
That percentile graded ladder of success
By releasing negative energy
We will all be one
And allow the full presence of GOD
In our minds, actions and words
It is poignant to know the truth
This requires working through and in the battle
Let our greatest gift partner with our mind
That is time
To conquer the opponent
May the most courageous win
May the hardworking win
May the true fighter win

HIGHLIGHT

"**By releasing negative energy**
We will all be one
And allow the full presence of GOD
In our minds, actions and words"

7-13-13
Inspired by my favorite book "Outwitting the devil" by Napoleon Hill

SO AND SO IS POISON

The collection of data
Given to our dear population
"The wired ones"
Is such a **dégât**
French for catastrophe
We are the ignorant ones
Who get the reruns…
This is so poisonous
Like a fish in a can
We need the speech of the brave
To fight against such a disgrace
Forget the news
It's all nuts
There are no values
Or people of guts
That can lead our way
Please inform us
Find the right things to say
Stand in front of the cause
And do it everyday
Tired of being misled
Am I the only one?
Tired of being misinformed
Am I the only one?
We are hidden the biggest secrets
And forced to make the biggest mistakes
We are facing the fakest faces
Behind the most appealing words
Promised the most impossible promises
That our box of expectations can't hold
We are so wired
We don't know it

When we know it
We get fired for it
Like the movies portray them
And we laugh
We taste whole for a change
But end up in half
We take the outcomes for granted
Those of entertainment are so demanded
Got to travel to that land
Be at the right place at the right time
But what for?
That news!!!
Big dollars in their pockets
Their mouth shall speak from A-F
Occasionally take M or R
But got to go back to A thru F
And forget the rest, or else
The job will be done
And someone will be away
From their family forever
But should they deliver it?
Why should they not?
Just told you
The population is so blind
Because of a collective narrow mind
Based on dependent personality
That cannot speak the truth
Speak the truth
For it shall set you free
It's the ultimate proof

HIGHLIGHT

"Like the movies portray them
And we laugh
We taste whole for a change
But end up in half"

07-31-09

STOP CONTROLLING ME...

I have my senses
The given ones at birth
That can help me help myself
I don't need a remote
For I'm not a TV
Don't change my channel
Because God is showing
Stop CONTROLLING me...

I have my senses
The given ones at birth
That tells me you're evil
That your eye's' fake
That your good is bad
Stop telling me what to do
Stop CONTROLLING me...

I have my senses
The given ones at birth
That tells me that your end is near
Don't worry for you deserve it
The mask shalt fall
You will stop fooling the world
And stop controlling me

HIGHLIGHT

**"Don't change my channel
Because God is showing"**

03-25-2010

GOD, YOU'RE SPEAKING

God You're speaking…
Through the Holy Spirit
Speaking so silently
I never felt so blessed
Hearing you
Through the man of your choice
Exalting with your powerful voice

God You're speaking…
Through the Holy Spirit
Speaking of my life
Guiding my own path
Healing my wounds
Your words are lighting my soul
Rendering clear my goal

Oh God You're speaking
Through the Holy Spirit
A divine language
One of comfort, strength and courage
In my thoughts, in my dreams
An unburdened heart I feel
I am set to follow your will

God You're speaking
God You're speaking
Oh God you're speaking
What a wonderful feeling!

4-15-13

PARADE OF BLESSINGS
WITH ONLY EYES TO SEE

It looked like the sky had taken over the world like a rain flood over a house. Earth was totally removed from the surface of the universe and a twin sister was born unlike the latter and full of energy. She looked like an angel without wings filled with dynamism and ready to take the role of a queen or mother also standing in a circular room. Unbelievably looking, I stood there miraculously as if I was living the dream of eternity with my eyes opened.

"Wow" I said with an astonished voice.

The assembly was standing in line like Christians waiting for communion looking at me as if I was a ghost from hell. I was the sudden intrusive "persona non grata" who was forbidden all the goods.

From afar, I could see a lot and by approaching realize their meaning or give my own interpretation. I saw a man coming towards me with countless virtues throwing them as if he was pouring sacred water over me. My body was an absolute reject of the effect. It was me against the twin sister.

Twin sister supports Earth in everything that she does. She is like the spirit that acts upon thee and makes it meaningful. Twin sister carries the necessary weapons to combat for the justice of the younger sister.

In a world like that of 'twin sister', earthlings were happy with themselves. It was like bathing in fresh water every day; for the older you were the younger you looked. Some words were no longer necessary such as the death association or negative ones. Every problem had a solution.

And I was still standing there looking at this little boy smiling, smiling as a baby who has just grown two teeth. The woman who cared forgave him because he had done wrong.

"I love you mom," he said.

I was there looking still but my vision was faded, faded by the saturation of sleep. I was almost there but this voice told me to come back because this road is not mine yet. "When you seek the opposite of hell, you are blessed and the man will befriend you".

I couldn't hear so I said what...they who are part of the assembly never said anything to me.

A few days later, my mother and brother joined the assembly like two new members of the navy. That's when I realized the meaning of my old time brother's dream about the gold door that was guarded by the angel that he was forbidden himself.

I also thought about all the other similar dreams and connected them all waiting for my sentence.

Unfortunately, I opened my eyes and thought I saw "twin sister" but realized that I am living in her little sister's house with spoiled fruits where I am a persona grata by default.

The sky had not taken over the world. Mother Earth is not related to "twin sister" but could use her as a role model and change the life of earthlings. The *parade* of blessings with *eyes* to see can't take us to paradise but just give us a taste of what it is.

7/12

An event of great significance is to come...

Understand or not, it will have an impact on humanity. I am sending my people to places where they should be as my will. Therefore, do not be afraid. Wherever you are is where I want you to be. It will be the defining moment that will shed light upon true believers, bring forth new believers and leave in the dark ignorant and stubborn people. In those times and especially at this very moment, everyone needs to pray not only for salvation but also for forgiveness. Mankind has gone too far with corrupted norms and truly needs repentance. I have spoken and will continue to speak to my servants of the plans already established. The devil has already built his empire on Earth and he is introducing many to his wicked deeds; but, I, the Lord, am here to remove my people from the mouth of the beast. All you need to do is pray fervently and accept that I am here to save you. I am a just God who is open to forgive all your sins but you have to be willing to come to Me. Remember I told you that everything that you are seeing in your surroundings was predicted to happen on the last days; time is nearer than ever and you must repent now. You, who believe, will understand and see my miracles as these things happen. I advise you to become a guide to those in the dark. Do not rejoice in the sufferings and ignorance of your close ones, family and friends. Again, I say; pray and pray for it is the key to salvation and the answer to your problems.

An event of great significance is to come...fight and death are involved. It is a defining event for humanity. Its outcome will impact humankind.

Holy Spirit Inspired

05-25-12

FINAL THOUGHTS

Time: We go through life knowing that time is money. It is rushing this hour and that hour. Well time is time; we cannot describe nor control it. The only thing we can control is what we do with it. Let's just let time be.

Money: We spend it and misspend it to buy what we don't need to impress people who don't even care about us as they usually say. Buy what you need, spend wisely on what you want, save for rainy days and invest for your future. You can check my bio for reference.

Style: Please guys…pull up the pants. Let's be more creative. The opposite of style has now become the style itself.

Fairness: The most heart pouring professions are the most underpaid and the ones that guide the world in the wrong direction are overly paid. The sun is the biggest star of all. It is so just that it shines on us all.

False Impression: Sometimes the best advice can come from someone of no particular pedigree. It's not so much the words you hear, but more so the intention behind them.

Cultural Habits: We live a fast-paced life where we have no time for our families. We label ourselves with trending terms. We used to cook as a family; now fast food is the ultimate dish. It is eaten at the same pace it is made.

Friendship: Don't count how many friends you have, instead count on the ones who are always there to support you when in need. A true friend steps in when the worst happens.

Love: Love as much as you can, love unconditionally. Love is above all. It's the reason why we're breathing.

God: God is love, he is calling you to love one and another, to draw near and put your trust in Him. Living a surrendered life and one of prayer will lead you to intimacy with Him.

Ending note: Life has its own purpose but what's your own purpose to make your journey promising in it.

W.O.R.D.S.

With wisdom and willingness you can achieve all that you want in life. First you need an objective and your obligation is to follow that objective. Reason and react immediately. The spirit in you will never fool you; it is here to guide you. Dream and dare to follow your dreams. What good is a dream if not pursued? How great is a dream if not followed? Suffer and survive from your suffering for it is temporary.

THE END

Printed in the United States
by Baker & Taylor Publisher Services